HORIZON
CARRÉ

Also available in this series:

Skyquake / Temblor de cielo
Arctic Poems / Poemas árticos
Equatorial & other poems

Selected Poems

Vicente Huidobro

Square Horizon
Horizon carré

Translated from French and Spanish by
Tony Frazer

Shearsman Books

First published in the United Kingdom in 2019 by
Shearsman Books
50 Westons Hill Drive
Emersons Green
BRISTOL
BS16 7DF

Shearsman Books Ltd Registered Office
30–31 St. James Place, Mangotsfield, Bristol BS16 9JB
(this address not for correspondence)

www.shearsman.com

ISBN 978-1-84861-651-6

Translations copyright © Tony Frazer, 2019.

The right of Tony Frazer to be identified as the translator
of this work has been asserted by him in accordance with the
Copyrights, Designs and Patents Act of 1988.
All rights reserved.

Acknowledgements

Horizon carré was originally published in Paris in 1917 by
Paul Birault. The text here is mostly based on the first edition
and on the *Obra poética* (2003) whenever clarification was required.

The Spanish versions in Section III are all by Huidobro himself,
and their texts are drawn from the *Obra poética*,
in which they were first brought together.

The translator wishes to convey his thanks to Timothy Adès,
whose skill as a translator of French saved him from a number
of embarrassing errors in this volume. Any errors that remain
are of course entirely the fault of the translator.

CONTENTS

	Introduction	7

I

16	Nouvelle chanson / New Song	17
18	Glace / Mirror	19
20	L'homme triste / The Sad Man	21
24	L'homme gai / The Happy Man	25
26	Automne / Autumn	27
28	Aveugle / Blind Man	29
30	Minuit / Midnight	31
32	Noir / Dark	33
34	Orage / Storm	35
38	Nouvel an / New Year	39
40	Tam / Tam	41
44	Vide / Empty	45
46	Âme / Soul	47

II

50	Chemin / Road/Path	51
53	Téléphone / Telephone	53
54	Pluie / Rain	55
56	Il neige / It's snowing	57
58	Voix / Voice	59
60	Calvaire / Calvary	61
62	Chanson / Song	63
64	Paysage / Landscape	65
66	Aéroplane / Aeroplane	69
70	Jardin / Garden	71
72	Drame / Drama	73
76	Tragédie / Tragedy	77
78	Oiseau / Bird	79
80	Hiver / Winter	81

82	Romance / Romance	83
84	Cowboy / Cowboy	85
86	Arc voltaique / Voltaic Arc	87
88	Rue / Street	89
90	Fable / Fable	91
92	Fleuve / River	93
94	Matin / Morning	95
96	Guitare / Guitar	97
98	Vates / Vates	99
100	Fin / End	101

Spanish Versions

106	Nueva Canción / New Song	107
108	Espejo / Mirror	109
110	El hombre triste / The Sad Man	111
114	El hombre alegre / The Happy Man	115
116	Paisaje / Landscape	117
118	[Aeroplano] / [Aeroplane]	119
120	Fábula / Fable	121
122	[Río] / [River]	123
124	Mañana / Morning	125
126	Guitarra / Guitar	127
128	Vates / Vates	129
130	Fin / End	131

	Notes	132

Vicente Huidobro and *Horizon Carré*

The Chilean poet Vicente Huidobro (1893-1948) is one of the most important figures in 20th-century Hispanic poetry and, along with César Vallejo, one of the pioneering avant-gardists in Spanish literature. Like Vallejo, he lived for many years in Paris but, unlike his Peruvian contemporary, he participated fully in the city's various artistic movements. Influenced initially by Apollinaire, whom he met within weeks of arriving in the city, Huidobro fell in early with forward-looking French writers such as Blaise Cendrars, Pierre Reverdy and Jean Cocteau.

Originally from an upper-class Santiago family, Huidobro was fortunate to have the means to support himself and his family while he found his artistic way, and—after an early phase in his native country writing in a quasi-symbolist style, influenced by Rubén Darío—he felt he had outgrown provincial Santiago.

He left Chile with his family in late 1916, bound first for Madrid, and then for Paris. While he very much wanted to see what was happening in the world's artistic capital, the initial impetus for the move had in fact been the avoidance of further scandal at home, where Huidobro had not long before gone off to Buenos Aires with Teresa Wilms Montt. The pair certainly had an affair, but the event also had a slightly more gentlemanly aspect, as Huidobro had engineered Teresa's escape from the Santiago convent in which she had been immured by her irate husband, following her affair with one of his cousins. Teresa was to develop her own literary career in Buenos Aires and would later move on to Europe, where she committed suicide in 1921. Huidobro continued to remember her long afterwards, and the daring escape to Argentina prefigured his later exploits with Ximena Amunátegui, who was to become his second wife.

* * *

Huidobro published *Horizon carré* in Paris in 1917, and quickly followed it with *El espejo de agua* (The Water Mirror, in Spanish, 2nd edition, Madrid, 1918), *Tour Eiffel* (Eiffel Tower, in French; Madrid, 1918), *Hallali* (in French; Madrid, 1918); *Ecuatorial* (Equatorial, in Spanish; Madrid, 1918) and *Poemas árticos* (Arctic Poems, likewise published in Spanish in Madrid, 1918). All of these are available in this series of books, *Arctic Poems* in one volume, and *Equatorial and other poems* containing the rest. These publications mark the beginning of the Huidobro's engagement with the European avant-garde, and a transition away from the influence of Rubén Darío that had dominated his early poetry.

Horizon carré is heavily influenced by the work of Guillaume Apollinaire and marks Huidobro's definitive arrival on the avant-garde scene in Paris, even if—it must be admitted—the volume is somewhat derivative. Huidobro's French was good even before he arrived in Paris; he had been educated well in Santiago, but this would not have prepared him for the linguistic and intellectual ferment he would find upon arrival in the main seat of the international avant-garde. Many of his early French-language manuscripts show signs of corrections by his friends at the time—Pierre Reverdy and the Spanish artist, Juan Gris, both being among them. Some of the poems in the book were reworked from Spanish poems in the chapbook collection, *El espejo de agua*, the resulting versions being given an Apollinairean *mise-en-page*. Huidobro was much taken with Apollinaire's *calligrammes* and composed several such poems himself, but he also adopted the freer organisation of text pioneered by the French poet.

Part and parcel of the intellectual ferment in which the poet found himself was the founding of the Creationism movement (*Creacionismo*). While this has been much discussed by critics, the fact is that Huidobro was just about its only "member". Gerardo Diego in Madrid was briefly involved, before moving on to the Ultraists; Cocteau, Radiguet and Reverdy were all published in the magazine *Creación / Création*. At the time, having an *-ism* was important; having a manifesto was important; both things piqued the interest of commentators and ensured that one was interviewed, ensured that one was taken seriously in the same way that the painters were taken seriously. Creationism is in some ways a literary analogue of Cubism, but there is nothing spectacularly original about it. The fact that it is still discussed seriously today proves, however, that a movement was worth founding. *Horizon carré* was a kind of calling-card for the new "movement", as can be seen by the epigraph to section 1, which sets out the creationist stall, so to speak.

* * *

Apart from the experimental French poets, Huidobro was also quickly drawn to the group of expatriate Spanish artists—Picasso and Juan Gris chief among them—together with the Cuban-French artist, Francis Picabia. Both Picasso and Gris drew portraits of Huidobro, and these contacts in the art world led him to close relationships with others, such as Jacques Lipchitz, Hans (Jean) Arp, and Robert Delaunay. The cultural ferment in Paris, the war notwithstanding, was something that Huidobro threw himself into with relish. He would soak up the exhibitions, the music—he also got to know members of *Les Six* as well as Edgard Varèse, the literary salons and café society. His work was marked by this forever, although he was to calm down in his artistic maturity after the great long works published in 1931 (*Altazor* and *Temblor de cielo*). He was also to move into other spheres, leaving some of this poetic experimentation behind, writing successful novels and stage works, repeatedly founding magazines that quickly folded, while also finding time to join the political fray back in Santiago and (temporarily) to run for President.

Like many intellectuals of his era he flirted with leftist politics, and joined the Communist Party—although he was to move away from them in later years, being unsatisfied with their dogma. He agitated in Madrid in the late 1930s for the republican government, against the insurrectionist forces of General Franco.

Huidobro's personal life also went through its ups and downs. During the early years in Paris he was accompanied by his wife, Manuela—like Vicente, a scion of a Chilean upper class family—and their children, two born in Chile, and two in Europe. In 1928 he dumped Manuela in favour of the barely-of-age Ximena Amunátegui, a relative by marriage, whom he whisked away from her boarding school in a dramatic escape to Argentina, whence the pair went to Paris. The couple went on to have one child, Vicente's last. Vicente had been in love with Ximena from 1926, when she was *not* of age—although it should be clarified here that there is no suggestion that the infatuation was anything other than platonic—and created an enormous scandal by announcing his love in a long poem that was published in the Santiago newspaper, *La Nación*. His marriage to Ximena officially lasted until 1945, when she requested a divorce; she then married a younger admirer, Godofredo Iommi (1917–2001)—also a poet, who had been a great admirer of Huidobro's work and had long been besotted with Ximena.

* * *

Portrait of Huidobro by Juan Gris, August 1917.

Octavio Paz later referred to Huidobro as *el oxígeno invisible* (the invisible oxygen) of Latin American poetry, reflecting the fact that his influence was felt by poets right across the continent; in fact he was probably *the* major link between the European avant-garde and progressive literary circles in Latin America.

    Huidobro was a restless soul and an artist of the very highest calibre. Today he is probably most revered for his extraordinary long poem *Altazor*, apparently written over a period of some 12 years and finally published in 1931. [There is an excellent translation of this work by Eliot Weinberger available from Wesleyan University Press.] Less well-known is the long prose poem *Temblor de cielo (Skyquake*—a translation of which is also available in this series), published the same year and mostly written in 1928. Huidobro regarded the two works as his artistic testament, and the summation of his work up to that point. He continued to look back fondly at his tyro works created in the early European years, however, and we need to understand them in order to appreciate how he reached the apotheosis represented by those great works of 1931.

Tony Frazer
January 2019

HORIZON CARRÉ

SQUARE HORIZON

À MADAME LUISA FERNÁNDEZ DE HUIDOBRO

I

Créer un poème en empruntant à la vie ses motifs et en les transformant pour leur donner une vie nouvelle et indépendante.

Rien d'anecdotique ni de descriptif. L'émotion doit naître de la seule vertu créatrice.

Faire un POÈME comme la nature fait un arbre.

FOR MADAME LUISA FERNÁNDEZ DE HUIDOBRO

I

To create a poem by borrowing its motifs from life and then transforming them so as to give them a new and independent life.

Nothing anecdotal, nothing descriptive. Emotion should be born of nothing but creative virtue.

To make a POEM as Nature makes a tree.

NOUVELLE CHANSON

POUR TOI MANUELITA

En dedans de l'Horizon
QUELQU'UN CHANTAIT
                    Sa voix
             N'est pas connue

                            D'OÙ VIENT-IL

Parmi les branches
On ne voit personne

La lune même était une oreille

Et on n'entend
              aucun bruit

             Cependant
                      une étoile déclouée
Est tombée dans l'étang

      L'HORIZON
                S'EST FERMÉ
Et il n'y a pas de sortie

NEW SONG

                                      FOR YOU MANUELITA

Inside the Horizon
SOMEONE WAS SINGING
                      His voice
                      Was unknown

                    WHERE DOES HE COME FROM

Among the branches
No one can be seen

The moon itself was an ear

And no sound
                can be heard

            However
                        an unhooked star
Has fallen into the pond

     THE HORIZON
              IS CLOSED
And there is no way out

GLACE

Ma   FACE
Et autour un peu d'eau

La glace
                               Et une porte ouverte
Qui montre une chambre pareille

SINGE
Pourquoi fais-tu ce que je fais
                               Je m'attends
                               derrière la glace

MIRROR

My FACE
And a little water around me

The mirror
      And an open door
That shows an identical room

MONKEY
Why do you do what I do
      I'm waiting for myself
     behind the mirror

L'HOMME TRISTE

Sur mon cœur
                il y a des voix qui pleurent

Ne plus penser à rien
Les souvenirs et la douleur se dressent
Prends garde aux portes mal fermées

                LES CHOSES S'ENNUIENT
Dans la chambre
Derrière la fenêtre où le jardin se meurt les feuilles pleurent
Et dans le foyer
                tout s'écrase
Tout est noir
Rien ne vit
        que dans les yeux du chat

SUR LA ROUTE
        UN HOMME S'EN VA
L'horizon parle
Et derrière on s'efface

La mère
        est morte sans rien dire
Et dans ma gorge un souvenir

THE SAD MAN

There are voices weeping
                              over my heart

No longer thinking of anything
Memories and pain stand erect
Beware of poorly-closed doors

              THINGS ARE BORED
In the room
Behind the window where the garden is dying leaves weep
And in the hearth
                            everything crashes

Everything is black
Nothing lives
               except in the cat's eyes

ON THE ROAD
            A MAN IS GOING AWAY
The horizon speaks
And beyond they vanish

The mother
               has died without saying a word
And in my throat a memory

TA FIGURE
                      au feu s'illumine
Quelque chose voudrait sortir

Quelqu'un tousse
                      dans l'autre chambre
UNE VIEILLE VOIX
                                Comme c'est loin
Un peu de mort tremble dans tous les coins

YOUR FACE
                      lit by the fire
Something would like to emerge

Someone coughs
                      in the other room
AN OLD VOICE
                                As if so far away
A little bit of death trembles in every corner

L'HOMME GAI

Il ne pleuvra plus
Mais quelques larmes encore
Brillent dans ta chevelure

UN HOMME SAUTE DANS LE SOLEIL

Ses yeux sont pleins de la poussière
                                        de tous les chemins
Et sa chanson ne pousse pas sur ses lèvres

Le jour se casse contre les vitres
Et les angoisses
                se sont évanouies
Le monde est plus clair
                que mon miroir
Le vol des oiseaux
                    et les cris des enfants
        Sont de la même couleur

PAR DESSUS LES ARBRES
            PLUS HAUTS QUE LE CIEL
On entend les cloches

THE HAPPY MAN

It won't rain any more
But some tears still
Shine in your tresses

A MAN JUMPS INTO THE SUN

His eyes are full of dust
                      from all the roads
And his song does not push past his lips

The day breaks against the windowpanes
And the disquiet
              has faded away
The world is clearer
              than my mirror
The flight of birds
                  and the cries of children
          Are the same colour

ABOVE THE TREES
         HIGHER THAN THE SKY
You can hear the bells

AUTOMNE

Je garde dans mes yeux
La chaleur de tes larmes
        Les dernières
Maintenant
      tu ne pourras pleurer
Jamais plus

  Par les chemins
       qui ne finissent pas
L'automne vient
Des doigts
       blancs de neige
Arrachent toutes les feuilles

       Quelle fatigue
  Le vent
      Le vent
UNE PLUIE D'AILES
    COUVRE LA TERRE

AUTUMN

In my eyes I retain
The heat of your tears
                                          The final ones
Now
                     you will not be able to weep
Ever again

      On roads
                                 that do not end
Autumn is coming
Fingers
                              white with snow
Snatch away all the leaves

                              What weariness
    The wind
                            The wind
A SHOWER OF WINGS
                    COVERS THE EARTH

AVEUGLE

Au delà de la dernière fenêtre
Les cloches du Sacré-Cœur
Font tomber les feuilles

    SUR LE SOMMET
            UN AVEUGLE

Les paupières pleines de musique
Lève les mains
            au milieu du vide

Celle qui vient de loin
Ne lui a pas donné son bras

Il est tout seul

            Et avec sa gorge coupée
Il chante une mélodie
        que personne
            n'a comprise

BLIND MAN

Beyond the last window
The bells of Sacré-Cœur
Make the leaves fall

    AT THE TOP
                A BLIND MAN

Eyelids full of music
Raise your hands
                amid the void

The woman who comes from afar
has not given him her arm

He is all alone

                And with his slashed throat
He sings a song
            that no-one
                  has understood

MINUIT

Les heures glissent
Comme des gouttes d'eau sur une vitre

                        Silence de minuit

La peur se déroule dans l'air
Et le vent
      se cache au fond du puits

      OH

    C'est une feuille
           On pense que la terre va finir
        Le temps
                  remue dans l'ombre
Tout le monde dort

                  UN SOUPIR

Dans la maison quelqu'un vient de mourir

MIDNIGHT

The hours slip by
Like drops of water on the windowpane

                                  Silence of midnight

Fear unfolds in the air
And the wind
                hides at the bottom of the well

            OH

      It's a leaf
                You'd think the world was ending
                Time
                          stirs in the shadow
Everyone sleeps

                      A SIGH

In the house someone has just died

NOIR

La chambre sans porte
On sent s'en aller la lumière
Les ombres
        sortent de sous les meubles
Les objets
        qu'on a perdus
                se rient

Le toit est presque un arbre
Et la lune regarde
        Parmi les branches

LA NATURE MORTE EST UN PAYSAGE

La nuit
La chambre s'inonde

        UN CRI
                PLEIN D'ANGOISSE

                Personne
                        ne m'a répondu

BLACK

The room with no door
You sense the light going
The shadows
                emerge from under the furniture
Objects
        that were lost
                laugh

The roof is almost a tree
And the moon watches
                Among the branches

THE STILL LIFE IS A LANDSCAPE

Night
The room is flooded

    A CRY
        FULL OF DESPAIR

            No-one
                has answered me

ORAGE

À MAX JACOB

Nuit de tempête
L'obscurité me mord la tête

Les diables
        cochers du tonnerre
                sont en vacances

Personne ne passe dans la rue
Elle n'est pas venue

Quelque chose
        est tombé dans le coin
Et la pendule
        ne bouge plus
VILLE   Parfois le trolley
       Fait s'envoler
                de petits oiseaux de feu

Dans la montagne
Les troupeaux   *CAMPAGNE*
      tremblent sous l'orage

Le chien boîteux qui surveille
Cherche son ombre

STORM

FOR MAX JACOB

A stormy night
The darkness bites my head

Devils
        thunder's coachmen
                      are on holiday

No-one passes in the street
She has not come

Something
        has fallen in the corner
And the pendulum
        no longer moves

TOWN   Occasionally the trolleybus
        Makes the little
                fire birds fly away

In the mountains
Flocks   *COUNTRYSIDE*
    tremble under the storm

The lame dog on guard
Looks for his own shadow

                    Viens plus près de moi
                        On fera un beau voyage
Dans le désert de l'Afrique
                    Les girafes veulent avaler la lune

Il ne faut pas regarder
                    derrière les murs
La curiosité allonge les cous

            On se cherche
            Et l'on ne trouve pas le chemin

Je cache un souvenir
Mais c'est inutile de regarder mes yeux

Autour de la maison
                le vent gronde

Peut-être là-bas ma mère
                        pleure

UN COUP DE TONNERRE FATIGUÉ
                S'est posé sur le plus haut sommet

     Come closer to me
     We'll have a good trip
In the African desert
     Giraffes want to swallow the moon

You must not look
     behind the walls
Curiosity makes necks longer

   We look for ourselves
   And do not find the way

I hide a memory
But it is useless to look into my eyes

All around the house
     the wind roars

Perhaps down there my mother
         is weeping

A WEARY THUNDERCLAP
   Has settled on the highest peak

NOUVEL AN

L'échelle de Jacob
                    n'était pas un rêve
Un œil s'ouvre devant la glace
Et les gens qui descendent
                    sur l'écran
Ont déposé leur chair
                    comme un vieux pardessus

    LE FILM 1916   *GUERRE*
        SORT D'UNE BOITE

La pluie tombe devant les spectateurs

Derrière la salle
UN VIEILLARD A ROULÉ DANS LE VIDE

NEW YEAR

Jacob's ladder
                was not a dream
An eye opens in front of the mirror
And the people who come down
                              on the screen
Have shed their flesh
                like an old overcoat

    THE FILM 1916   *WAR*
        EMERGES FROM A BOX

The rain falls before the spectators

Behind the hall
AN OLD MAN HAS ROLLED INTO THE VOID

TAM

À PAUL DERMÉE

Chanter
        le soir sur les monts
En regardant passer les aéroplanes
            Oiseaux de l'horizon
Qui s'allaitent à la lune

J'ai soif
Donnez-moi à boire
            Toutes les blondes chevelures
Dans le silence
On sent s'enfuir quelques souvenirs

    Gibier à la débandade
Comment les saisir

Personne n'a pu arrêter ma marche
Le soleil brille
       La vie est bonne
Et ton souvenir chante dans ma montre

    Le vieux Tam
          Dans un feu follet
Allume son cigare
Et s'éloigne en chantant par le bois

TAM

FOR PAUL DERMÉE

Singing
            this evening on the hills
Watching the aeroplanes go by
              Birds on the horizon
Suckling at the moon

I'm thirsty
Give me something to drink
                    All the blonde tresses
In the silence
You can sense some memories fleeing

      Game-birds in a mad rush
How to catch them

No-one could stop my progress
The sun is shining
          Life is good
And your memory sings in my wristwatch

      Old Tam
             In a will o'the wisp
Lights his cigar
And moves away singing through the wood

Tu seras
              toute la lumière
                              cette nuit

Les marionnettes qui pendent
Aux rayons des étoiles
Sont des araignées

   DANSE
              VIEUX TAM
                            DANSE
Au milieu des sept enfants de la montagne

Dans la main prends
Celui qui joue de la flûte

TA
    TÊTE
        PEND
            DE LA
                FUMÉE
                    DE TON
                          CIGARE

You will be
                all the light
                              tonight

The dolls which hang
On star beams
Are spiders

    DANCE
                OLD TAM
                            DANCE
Amidst the seven children from the mountain

Take him by the hand
The one playing the flute

YOUR
      HEAD
          HANGS
              FROM THE
                    SMOKE
                         OF YOUR
                                  CIGAR

VIDE

À BLAISE CENDRARS

La chanson qui monte
Est devenue une étoile
          Par dessous la porte
          L'âme de la chambre
          s'était échappée
  Maison vide
Le jardin s'ennuie
          Aucun bruit
Aucune lampe ne s'allume

L'arbre est un balai

Il y a quelque temps
          Les murs
Ont écouté de belles paroles
Un soupir avait terni le miroir

La morte qu'on a emportée l'autre jour
Etait si jeune et si douce

          IL FAIT FROID

Les cheminées sans feu tremblotent
Le plancher craque

LA GLACE
      s'ennuie d'attendre

EMPTY

FOR BLAISE CENDRARS

The rising song
has become a star
                  From under the door
                  The room's soul
                  had escaped
    Empty house
The garden is bored
                No sound
No lamp is lit

The tree is a broom

Some time ago
                The walls
Listened to fine words
A sigh had tarnished the mirror

The dead woman who was carried off the other day
Was so young and so sweet

                    IT'S COLD

The hearths with no fire are shivering
The floor creaks

THE MIRROR
                is bored with waiting

ÂME

À SOLER CASABON

Quelque chose frôle le mur

Mais l'âme qui pourrait naître

N'a pas d'yeux

Celle qui cherche une porte

                       Demain regardera

Le bruit de ses pas

                    S'est noyé dans le tapis

On ne trouve pas

Dans la vie

           Il y a quelque fois un peu de soleil

    ELLE VIENDRA

                ON L'ATTEND

SOUL

FOR SOLER CASABON

Something brushes the wall

But the soul that might be born

Has no eyes

The woman looking for a door

                             Will watch tomorrow

The sound of her footsteps

                      drowns in the carpet

It's not to be found

In life

         There is sometimes a little sunshine

       SHE WILL COME

                     WE'RE WAITING FOR HER

II

À JUAN GRIS

II

FOR JUAN GRIS

CHEMIN

TON CRI
        Perça le plafond
Et la pluie sur ton visage
Le délaye dans l'ombre
              OÙ VAS-TU

Le chemin de la glace
Est long à parcourir
Et les cheminées
            font l'adieu des mouchoirs

ELLE S'EST NOYÉE DANS LE MIROIR

Les saules de la rive
        méditent

PATH

YOUR CRY
           Pierced the ceiling
And the rain on your face
Reduces it in the shadow
                  WHERE ARE YOU GOING

The path on the ice
Is a long way to travel
And the hearths
              bid farewell with handkerchiefs

IT HAS DROWNED IN THE MIRROR

The willows on the bank
              are meditating

TÉLÉPHONE

FILS TÉLÉPHONIQUES
CHEMIN DES MOTS

                        Et dans la nuit
                        Violon de la lune

                UNE VOIX

Une montagne
                s'est levée devant moi
Ce qui attend derrière
                cherche son chemin

DEUX ENDROITS
                DEUX OREILLES

    Une route longue à parcourir

Paroles
        le long de ton cheveu
Une est tombée à l'eau

ALLÔ
                          ALLÔ

TELEPHONE

TELEPHONE LINES
PATH FOR WORDS

                        And in the night
                        the moon's violin

                            A VOICE

A mountain
            has risen up before me
What waits beyond
                  looks for its path

TWO PLACES
                      TWO EARS

   A long road to travel

Words
        the length of your hair
One of them has fallen into the water

HELLO
                            HELLO

PLUIE

À PIERRE REVERDY

UN BRAS INCONNU
                         a levé le soleil
                         parmi la pluie
Soleil montagnard
Ce matin est plus tard que d'habitude
Une cloche a lancé à l'eau
                         toutes les heures
Mais nous sortirons le soir
                         chercher l'aventure

         MOURIR
                 À CHAQUE COIN

La lanterne sourde
                 éclaire
                         ma main vide
Où il n'y a que
                         4
                     DOIGTS

RAIN

FOR PIERRE REVERDY

AN UNKNOWN ARM
                      has raised the sun
                      amidst the rain
Mountain sun
This morning is later than usual
A bell has thrown all the hours
                          into the water
But we'll go out this evening
                seeking adventure

    DYING
            IN EVERY CORNER

The deaf lantern
        illuminates
                my empty hand
Where there are only
                  4
              FINGERS

IL NEIGE

À IGOR STRAVINSKI

LA FEMME
        QUI JOUAIT DU VIOLON
                Dort

Dans ses yeux vides
        rien que des larmes
Il était l'hiver
        dans un coin du miroir
Et les notes
        qui tombaient à moitié chemin
N'avaient pas d'ailes
        comme ses paupières

LE VIOLON
        SAIGNE SUR LA NEIGE

IT'S SNOWING

FOR IGOR STRAVINSKY

THE WOMAN
            WHO WAS PLAYING THE VIOLIN
                        Is sleeping

In her empty eyes
            nothing but tears

It was winter
            in one corner of the mirror

And the notes
            which fell half way

Had no wings
            like her eyelids

THE VIOLIN
            BLEEDS ON THE SNOW

VOIX

CELUI QUI POURRAIT
    CHANTER
        N'a pas de gosier

Son cri d'angoisse
Noyé dans le bois feutré

DERRIÈRE SA TÊTE
    LE BORD DU MONDE

En levant un pied
    il tomberait dans le vide

POURTANT SES LARMES
    LE SAUVERONT

VOICE

THAT MAN WHO MIGHT
                            SING
                                          Has no throat

His cry of despair
Drowns in the muffled wood

BEHIND HIS HEAD
                        THE EDGE OF THE WORLD

If he raised a foot
                        he would fall into the void

HOWEVER HIS TEARS
                      WILL SAVE HIM

CALVAIRE

La voiture oscillait
                sur la montagne invisible

Quelqu'un cherchait des perles
Parmi les empreintes des loups

ET SEULES
        QUELQUES GOUTTES ROUGES

Un abîme se cachait au milieu des nuages
Et toujours du sang
                sur les chemins de plâtre

On a crucifié le Christ
                Là-haut sur le sommet

CALVARY

The car swayed
                on the invisible mountain

Someone was searching for pearls
Among the tracks of wolves

AND ONLY
        SOME RED DROPS

An abyss was hidden amongst the clouds
And always blood
                on the plaster paths

Christ was crucified
                    Up there on the peak

CHANSON

Quelqu'un
                que tu n'es pas
Chante derrière le mur

Le miroir
                dédoublait la voix
Et des étoiles naufragées
                        Dormaient sur tes sens

QUI ES-TU

                    La voix qui a répondu
Venait de plus loin que ta poitrine

SONG

Someone
            who isn't you
Is singing behind the wall

The mirror
            doubled the voice
And shipwrecked stars
              Slept on your senses

WHO ARE YOU

              The voice that replied
Came from somewhere beyond your breast

PAYSAGE

À PABLO PICASSO

LE SOIR ON SE PROMÈNERA SUR DES ROUTES PARALLÈLES

La lune

où

tu te regarde

L'ARBRE
ÉTAIT
PLUS
HAUT
QUE LA
MONTAGNE

MAIS LA
MONTAGNE   LE
ÉTAIT SI LARGE   FLEUVE
QU'ELLE DÉPASSAIT   QUI
LES EXTRÉMITÉS   COULE
DE LA TERRE   NE
                        PORTE
                           PAS
                              DE
                                 POISSONS

ATTENTION À NE PAS
JOUER SUR L'HERBE
FRAÎCHEMENT PEINTE

UNE CHANSON CONDUIT LES BREBIS VERS L'ÉTABLE

LANDSCAPE

FOR PABLO PICASSO

THIS EVENING WE WILL WALK ON PARALLEL ROADS

The moon where you watch yourself

        THE TREE
        WAS
        TALLER
        THAN
        THE
        MOUNTAIN

BUT THE
  MOUNTAIN   THE
WAS SO VAST   RIVER
THAT IT SURPASSED WHICH
THE VERY ENDS   WINDS
OF THE EARTH   BY
                    CARRIES
                        NO
                          FISH

        BEWARE DO NOT PLAY
        ON THE GRASS
        IT'S FRESHLY PAINTED

A SONG LEADS THE SHEEP TO THE BYRE

AÉROPLANE

Une croix
            s'est abattue par terre

Un cri brisa les fenêtres
Et on se penche
            sur le dernier aéroplane

Le vent
        qui avait nettoyé l'air
A naufragé dans les premières vagues

La poussée
            persiste encore
                      sur les nuages

Et le tambour
            appelle quelqu'un
Que personne ne connaît

Des mots
          derrière les arbres

La lanterne qu'on agitait
                    était un drapeau
Il éclaire autant que le soleil

AEROPLANE

A cross
        has been shot down

A cry broke the windows
And you can lean
        over the last aeroplane

The wind
        which had cleansed the air
Has been wrecked on the first waves

The impulse
        still persists
                among the clouds

And the drum
        calls to someone
That no-one knows

Words
        behind the trees

The lamp being shaken
            was a flag
It gave as much light as the sun

Mais les cris qui enfoncent les toits
                        ne sont pas de révolte
Malgré les murs qui ensevelissent

        LA CROIX DU SUD

Est le seul avion
              qui subsiste

But the cries that hammer on the roofs
                            are from no uprising
Despite the walls that shroud them

      THE SOUTHERN CROSS

Is the only aircraft
                      that survives

JARDIN

Une voix sortie de l'armoire
Aurait ému le cœur
Et tout ce qui tombe
                contre le mur
Est d'une pureté inconnue

Dans le jardin
          à peine coloré
Les arbres refusent l'ombre
                      Que donnent
                les statues

Et les doigts
          qui tombent
                    entre les feuilles
Craquent sur le sable

Le chat
       tiédit au soleil
                endormi sur le lac

GARDEN

A voice coming from the wardrobe
Touched your heart it seems
And all that falls
                against the wall
Is of an unknown purity

In the garden
                barely coloured
The trees refuse the shade
                          Given by
                    statues

And the fingers
                that fall
                      amongst the leaves
Creak on the sand

The cat
        basks in the sun
                  sleeping on the lake

DRAME

La nuit
        est descendue plus bas que d'habitude

L'ombre des chiens
Faisait craquer le sable

La fumée des pipes
        cache les voleurs

    Des mots
        parmi les buissons
  La maison
      est une île
          dans le vent

Et la peur grogne autour
Dans la chambre
        on tremble

La mère
    sous l'étoile qui troue le plafond
Ecrit au père
        déjà mort

DRAMA

Night
        has come down lower than usual

The shadow of dogs
Made the sand creak

Pipe-smoke
        hides the thieves

    Words
              amongst the bushes
The house
        is an island
              in the wind

And fear is growling round
In the room
              there's trembling

Mother
    under the star that bores through the ceiling
Writes to the father
              dead by now

DANS LA CHEMINÉE
    LES MARIONNETTES
        GRELOTTENT

THÉÂTRE

ON THE MANTELPIECE
THE DOLLS
SHIVER

THEATRE

TRAGÉDIE

À ERIK SATIE

Je marche au bord de la rivière
Un oiseau à ressort
                    chante à mon oreille

Sur le pont
             qui ne rejoint pas l'autre rive
Des gens
        habillés de noir
                cherchent avec des lanternes
L'aveugle
        dont les yeux
                sont plus froids que la lune

CELUI QUI RIT
        Se cache sous l'eau

Le lendemain
        à la surface du fleuve
On trouva un cercueil d'enfant

En ouvrant sa boîte à violon
                S'envola
            sa dernière chanson

TRAGEDY

FOR ERIK SATIE

I walk on the riverbank
A spring-loaded bird
                sings in my ear

On the bridge
         which does not reach the other bank
People
      dressed in black
               search with lanterns
The blind man
        whose eyes
               are colder than the moon

THE LAUGHING MAN
            Hides under the water

The next day
        floating on the river
A child's coffin was found

Upon opening his violin case
                His last song
           flew away

OISEAU

Parmi les vagues crémantes
La barque se berçait

    Un enfant chante
        dans le brouillard
LE PRINTEMPS
      NE REVIENDRA PLUS

Mais il y a encore des feuilles
Et
    quelque part
        on voit un nid
Balancé par des mains végétales

Un oiseau de neige
      s'apprend à chanter
Sur le dernier mât

BIRD

Amid the foaming waves
The boat was rocking

      A child sings
             in the fog
SPRINGTIME
         WILL NOT RETURN

But there are still some leaves
And
      somewhere
            a nest can be seen
Cradled by vegetal hands

A snow bird
      learns to sing
On the mizzen mast

HIVER

Je ne pourrais plus chanter
On m'a volé mes chansons

Dans ma gorge
                reste un goût de mélodie

La bûche qui flambe
                était une flûte
Elle chante l'hiver
                parmi d'autres branches

Souvenirs des aïeux   La résignation courbée
    tiédissant   regarde le sol
    près du feu   qui se dérobe

DANS LE JARDIN
                SANS OISEAUX

Le miroir d'eau
            s'est brisé

WINTER

I could not sing
My songs have been stolen

In my throat
                remains the taste of melody

The burning log
                was a flute
It sang winter
                among other branches

Memories of ancestors   Downcast resignation
    warming   watches the soil
    by the fire   undressing

IN THE GARDEN
                WITH NO BIRDS

The water mirror
                is broken

ROMANCE

L'oiseau
    qui s'est noyé dans tes larmes
chante encore
Et toi
   qui n'as jamais parlé
      Toi
        qui n'as pas de voix

Et qui es debout
      sur les quatre points cardinaux

   OÙ TOURNER
        SES YEUX

Le dernier souvenir
Tombera
   dans
     l'abîme
       sans
         mirage

APRÈS
   VÊTUS DE DEUIL
SANS MÊME REGARDER LES FEUILLES

ROMANCE

The bird
        which drowned in your tears
still sings
And you
        who have never spoken
                You
                        who have no voice

And who stands
        at the four points of the compass

    WHICH WAY
            TO LOOK

The last memory
Will fall
        into
            the abyss
                with no
                      mirage

AFTERWARDS
        IN MOURNING CLOTHES
NOT EVEN LOOKING AT THE LEAVES

COWBOY

À JACQUES LIPCHITZ

Sur le Far West
                 où il y a une seule lune
Le Cow Boy chante
                 à rompre la nuit
Et son cigare est une étoile filante

    SON POULAIN FERRÉ D'AILES
    N'A JAMAIS EU DE PANNE
Et lui
        la tête contre le genoux
                 danse un Cake Walk

New York
       à quelques kilomètres

Dans les gratte-ciels
Les ascenseurs montent comme des thermomètres

Et près du Niagara
                qui a éteint ma pipe
Je regarde les étoiles éclaboussées

Le Cow Boy
        sur une corde à violon
Traverse l'Ohio

COWBOY

FOR JACQUES LIPCHITZ

In the Wild West
                   where there is only one moon
The Cowboy sings
                   to split the night
And his cigar is a shooting star

    HIS COLT SHOD WITH WINGS
    HAS NEVER BROKEN DOWN
And he
         head against his knees
                   dances a Cakewalk

New York
        a few kilometres away

In the skyscrapers
The elevators climb like thermometers

And near Niagara
             which douses my pipe
I look at the bespattered stars

The Cowboy
        on a violin string
Crosses the Ohio

ARC VOLTAIQUE

La lumière
              en sortant de sa tête
       Ne se répand pas en lignes droites

              En dehors du cercle blanc
              Il se passe des drames lamentables

JE NE VOIS PAS
            LA VILLE
                  OÙ
                        SOMMES
                              NOUS

Des cris se noyent
                dans la mer épaisse
Et toutes les embarcations
                      s'en retournaient

Les rayons de lumière
                    qui tombent
Ont criblé le sol

VOLTAIC ARC

The light
        on leaving his head
     Does not spill out in straight lines

              Outside the white circle
              Pitiful dramas take place

I DO NOT SEE
              THE TOWN
                          WHERE
                                      ARE
                                                WE

Cries drowning
                in the deep sea
And all the boats
                returning

The falling
              beams of light
Have sifted the soil

RUE

À LOUIS DE GONZAGUE FRICK

Dans la rue
                qui finit sur le vide
    Seule ma pipe
                    chauffe mes mains
Et ma tête s'éloigne de mon corps

LA FEMME AUX SEINS MÛRS

Était dans le cercle lumineux
Cherchant ses yeux

Sur le trottoir
                qui tremble comme un pont
J'ai laissé ma chevelure

STREET

FOR LOUIS DE GONZAGUE FRICK

In the street
                  that ends in emptiness
    Only my pipe
                        warms my hands
And my head extends from my body

THE WOMAN WITH RIPE BREASTS

Was in the luminous circle
Looking for her eyes

On the pavement
                which sways like a bridge
I have left my hair

FABLE

Le chien qui avait mordu son ombre
Saignait dans le ruisseau

    Le vent
        enleva de sa tête
        quelques larmes d'oiseau

En léchant son ombre
Parfois il regarde les astres vieillis
        où tournoient des papillons

    Il sait que l'étoile des Rois Mages
    Etait un chien d'aveugle

FABLE

The dog that bit its shadow
Bled in the stream

    The wind
            wiped from its head
            some birds' tears

When licking its shadow
Perhaps it looks at the ancient stars
            where butterflies whirl

    It knows that the star of the Three Magi
    Was a blind man's dog

FLEUVE

À JEAN COCTEAU

Le Fleuve où le vent
              traîne des chansons

    VIEILLE VOIX MARINIÈRE

Les saules	Des femmes
qui écoutent	qui lavent
penchés	leurs chevelures

Le soleil en trouant les branches
Passe de l'autre côté
              sans arracher les feuilles
Il y a des dentelles sur l'eau
Mais L'OMBRE EST DOUCE à supporter

Le bras d'eau cherche l'horizon
Au fond du paysage

RIVER

FOR JEAN COCTEAU

The River where the wind
                      drags its songs

    OLD SAILOR'S VOICE

The willows   Women
that listen   who wash
bowed   their tresses

By piercing the branches the sun
Passes to the other side
                      without tearing off leaves
There's lacework on the water
But THE SHADOW IS TENDERLY borne

The water's arms search the horizon
At the landscape's end

MATIN

SOLEIL

Qui réveille Paris

S O L E I L   *Le plus haut peuplier de la rive*   Sur la Tour Eiffel   S O L E I L

Un coq à trois couleurs
Chante en battant des ailes
Et quelques plumes en tombent

En recommençant sa course
La Seine cherche entre les ponts
Sa vieille route

        Et l'Obélisque
        Qui a oublié les mots égyptiens
        Na pas fleuri cette année

SOLEIL

Morning

SUN

Which awakens Paris

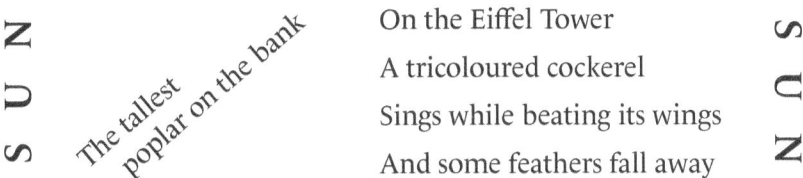

S U N   *The tallest poplar on the bank*   On the Eiffel Tower   S U N
A tricoloured cockerel
Sings while beating its wings
And some feathers fall away

On starting its course again
The Seine searches amongst the bridges
For its old route

                 And the Obelisk
                 Which has forgotten the Egyptian words
                 has not flowered this year

SUN

GUITARE

À HENRI LAURENS

Sur ses genoux
                Il y avait quelques notes

Une femme petite dormait
Et six cordes chantent
                dans son ventre

Le vent
       a effacé les contours
              Et un oiseau
           becquette les cordes

Le silence   Chacun croit
se cachait   vivre   en
au fond de   dehors   de
l'armoire   soi - même

Quand l'homme
            cessa de jouer
Deux ailes tremblotantes
                tombèrent de ses mains

GUITAR

FOR HENRI LAURENS

On his knees
                There were some notes

A small woman was sleeping
And six strings sing
                in her stomach

The wind
        has erased the contours
                      And a bird
                pecks the strings

The silence	All of us
hid itself	believe we
at the bottom	live outside
of the Wardrobe	ourselves

When the man
           stopped playing
Two fluttering wings
              fell from his hands

VATES

À GUILLAUME APOLLINAIRE

Le rosier qui pousse dans ma main
S'est effeuillé
Comme un vieux livre
Astres tombant
         sur la flaque d'eau

         Mais toi
                poète
           Tu as une étoile mûre
           Entre tes mains
           Et tes lèvres
           Sont encore humides
           De ses fils de miel

Une chanson
Electrise les eaux

Dans l'étang brisé
S'est noyé le dernier oiseau

Mais quand le printemps viendra
L'arbre du jardin
Fleurira d'yeux
         comme une canne d'aveugle

VATES

FOR GUILLAUME APOLLINAIRE

The rosebush that grows in my hand
Has been plucked
Like an old book
Stars falling
        on the puddle of water

              But you
                      poet
             You have a ripe star
             In your hands
             And your lips
             Are still moist
             From its honeyed threads

A song
thrills the waters

In the wrecked pond
The last bird has drowned

But when springtime comes
The tree in the garden
Will flower with eyes
            like a blind man's cane

Et toi
        poète
Tu portes à ta boutonnière

LA ROSE DES VENTS

And you
> poet

In your buttonhole you wear

THE WIND ROSE

FIN

La neige qui tombe
A blanchi quelques barbes

        Ses yeux à moitié ouverts
        Sont des morceaux de verre
        Mais il reste encore
        Un peu de feu

En arrivant   **S**
        la mort   **I**
                                           L
Coupe la dernière syllabe   **E**
Et tous ceux qui pleuraient   **N**
Allèrent se dispersant   **C**
                                           E

Au long du chemin
                Il y a des étoiles effeuillées

Et les feux follets
                Qui s'éloignent entre les branches
Laissent une odeur de cigare

                                      S I L E N C E

END

The falling snow
Has whitened some beards

        His half-open eyes
        Are pieces of glass
        But there is still
        A little fire left

When it arrives
        death
Cuts short the final syllable
And all those who wept
Were scattered

                      S
                      I
                      L
                      E
                      N
                      C
                      E

Along the path
        There are plucked stars

And the will o'the wisps
        In retreat among the branches
Leave behind the smell of cigars

                SILENCE

VERSIONS ESPAGNOLES

VERSIONES ESPAÑOLAS

SPANISH VERSIONS

NUEVA CANCIÓN

Dentro del horizonte
ALGUIEN CANTABA
                          Su voz no es conocida
           DE DÓNDE VIENE

Entre las ramas
No se ve a nadie

Hasta la luna era una oreja
Y no se oye
              ningún ruido

              Sin embargo
                      Una estalla desclavada
Ha caído en el estanque
       EL HORIZONTE
              SE HA CERRADO
Y no hay otra salida

NEW SONG

Inside the Horizon

SOMEONE WAS SINGING

                                       His voice is unknown

                   WHERE DOES HE COME FROM

Among the branches

No one can be seen

The moon itself was an ear
And no sound
                 can be heard

                     However
                            an unfixed star
Has fallen into the pond

       THE HORIZON
                 IS CLOSED
And there is no other way out

ESPEJO

Mi cara

Y en torno un poco de agua

El espejo

                Y una puerta abierta

Que muestra otra pieza igual

MONO

Por qué haces todo lo que yo hago

                              Yo me espero
                              detrás del espejo

MIRROR

My face
And around it a little water

The mirror
              And an open door
That shows an identical room

MONKEY

Why do you do everything I do

                        I'm waiting for myself
                        behind the mirror

EL HOMBRE TRISTE

Lloran voces sobre mi corazón
No más pensar en nada

Despierta el recuerdo y el dolor
Tened cuidado
           con las puertas mal cerradas

   LAS COSAS SE FATIGAN

En la alcoba
Detrás de la ventana
              donde el jardín se muere

           las hojas lloran

Y en la chimenea
            todo se abate
Todo es oscuro
Nada vive
          sino en los ojos del gato

SOBRE LA RUTA
           UN HOMBRE SE ALEJA
El horizonte habla
Y detrás se borran

THE SAD MAN

Voices weep over my heart
No longer thinking of anything

Awaken memory and pain
Beware
        of poorly-closed doors

   THINGS ARE WEARY

In the bedroom
Behind the window
               where the garden is dying

           leaves weep

And in the hearth
              everything is shattered
Everything is dark
Nothing lives
        except in the cat's eyes

ON THE ROAD
            A MAN IS GOING AWAY
The horizon speaks
And afterwards they fade away

La madre
    que murió sin decir nada
Trabaja en mi garganta
TU FIGURA
    El fuego la ilumina
Alguna cosa quisiera salir
Alguien tose en la otra pieza
UNA VOZ VIEJA
     Qué lejos
Un poco de muerte
    tiembla en los rincones

The mother
                who died without saying a word
Works in my throat
YOUR FACE
                The fire illuminates it
Something would like to emerge
Someone coughs in the other room
AN OLD VOICE
                      How far away it is
A little bit of death
                trembles in the corners

EL HOMBRE ALEGRE

No lloverá más
Pero algunas lágrimas
Brillan aún en tu cabellera

UN HOMBRE SALTA EN EL SOL

Sus ojos
        llenos del polvo de todos los caminos
Y su canción
            no brota de sus labios
El día se rompe contra los vidrios
Y las angustias se desvanecen
El mundo
      es más claro que mi espejo
El vuelo de los pájaros
                y el gritar de los niños
    Es del mismo color
SOBRE LOS ÁRBOLES
            MÁS ALTOS QUE EL CIELO
Se oye las campanas

THE HAPPY MAN

It won't rain any more
But some tears
Still shine in your tresses

A MAN JUMPS INTO THE SUN

His eyes
        full of dust from all the roads
And his song
            does not spring from his lips
The day breaks against the windowpanes
And the anxieties fade away
The world
        is clearer than my mirror
The flight of birds
            and the cries of children
    Are the same colour
ABOVE THE TREES
        HIGHER THAN THE SKY
You can hear the bells

PAISAJE

La luna donde tú te miras

El árbol
era más alto
que la
montaña

Pero la montaña   El
era tan ancha   río
que depasaba   que
las extremidades de la tierra   corre
 no lleva
 peces

 Cuidado no jugar
 sobre le yerba
 recién pintada

una canción conduce las ovejas al establo

LANDSCAPE

(The moon where you watch yourself)

        The tree
        was taller
        than the
        mountain

    But the mountain   The
    was so broad   river
    that it exceeded   that
the very ends of the earth   flows
                              carries no
                                    fish

                            Beware don't play
                            on the grass
                            it's recently painted

a song leads the sheep to the byre

[AEROPLANO]

El último aeroplano
                      se abatió contra la tierra
Un grito trizó las ventanas
Y en el rincón más oscuro
                      Se inclinaban sobre el muerto
El viento
Que había limpiado el aire
              ha naufragado
              en las primeras olas
El impulso persiste entre las nubes
El redoble del tambor
Llama a alguien que nadie conoce
Varias voces discutían
                    Detrás de los árboles
     La linterna que se agitaba
     Era una bandera
Se diría que iluminaba
              Tanto como el sol
Les gritos que surgían
              No eran de protesta
Uno a uno los muros
                  fueron cayendo
La Cruz del Sur
                Es el único avión que subsiste

[AEROPLANE]

The last aeroplane
    has been shot down
A cry broke the windows
And in the darkest corner
    They bent over the dead man
The wind
Which had cleansed the air
   has been wrecked
    on the first waves
The impulse persists among the clouds
The drum-roll
Calls to someone that no-one knows
Several voices argued
    Behind the trees
  The lamp being shaken
  Was a flag
It was said that it gave
    As much light as the sun
The cries that burst out
   Were no protest
One by one the walls
    were falling
The Southern Cross
   Is the only aircraft that survives

FÁBULA

El perro que había mordido su sombra
Sangraba en el arroyo
El viento al pasar
Quitó de su cabeza las lágrimas
                de un pájaro

Lamiendo su sombra
De cuando en cuando aúlla
Y mira los astros marchitos
Donde giran algunas mariposas

Él sabe que la estrella de los Magos
Era más fiel que un perro de ciego

FABLE

The dog that bit its shadow
Bled in the stream
In passing the wind
Wiped from its head the tears
                of a bird

Licking its shadow
From time to time it howls
And looks at the faded stars
Where some butterflies whirl around

It knows that the star of the Magi
Was more faithful than a blind man's dog

[RÍO]

El río o el viento
                arrastra algunas canciones
Vieja voz marinera
Los sauces   Son mujeres
que se inclinan   lavando
a escuchar   su cabellera

El sol agujereaba la ramas
Y pasa del otro lado
                  sin arrancar las hojas
Hay algunos encajes sobre el agua
Pero la sombra es dulce a soportar

El río
Es un brazo extendido que busca el horizonte
                                al fondo del paisaje

[RIVER]

The river or the wind
                        drags some songs along
Old sailor's voice
The willows   Are women
that bend over   washing
while they listen   their tresses

The sun pierced the branches
And passes through from the other side
                        without tearing off leaves
There's some lacework on the water
But the shadow is tenderly borne

The river
Is an outstretched arm searching the horizon
                                  at the landscape's end

MAÑANA

S O L

París después de dormir bien
Se desprereza

           Sobre la Torre Eiffel
           Un gallo de tres colores
           Canta en batiendo las alas
           Y caen algunas plumas

SOL Empezando a correr de nuevo
      El Sena busca entre los puentes
      Su vieja ruta   SOL

           El Obelisco todavía de pie
           Que ha olvidado la lengua egipcia
           No ha florido este año

S O L

MORNING

S U N

After sleeping well Paris
Shakes itself

          On the Eiffel Tower
          A tricoloured cockerel
          Sings while beating its wings
          And some feathers fall away

S U N   On starting its course again   S U N
       The Seine searches amongst the bridges
       For its old route

          Still standing erect the Obelisk
          That has forgotten the Egyptian language
          Has not flowered this year

S U N

GUITARRA

Sobre las rodillas
               había algunas notas
Una mujer pequeña dormía
Y seis cuerdas cantan
             en su vientre
El viento
       ha borrado los contornos

             Y un pájaro
      picotea las cuerdas

El silencio
Se escondía
Al fondo
Del armario

Cada una cree
vivir
fuera de
sí-mismo

Cuando el hombre dejó de tocar

Dos alas temblorosas
cayeron de sus manos

GUITAR

On his knees
                there were some notes
A small woman slept
And six strings sing
                in her stomach
The wind
      has erased the contours

                      And a bird
              pecks at the strings

Silence   Everyone believes
Hides away   he lives
At the bottom   outside of
Of the wardrobe   himself

When the man stopped playing

Two fluttering wings
fell from his hands

VATES

El rosal que crece en mi mano
Se ha deshojado
          como un viejo libro

                  Pero tú poeta
                  tienes aún
                  un astro maduro entre los manos
                  Y tus labios
                  están todavía húmedos
                  de sus hilos de miel

Una canción
Electriza las aguas

Y en el estanque trizado
Se ha ahogado el último pájaro

                  Tú poeta
                  La rosa de los vientos

VATES

The rosebush that grows in my hand
Has been plucked
            like an old book

                    But poet you
                    still have
                    a ripe star in your hands
                    And your lips
                    are still moist
                    from its honeyed threads

A song
Thrills the waters

And in the wrecked pond
The last bird has drowned

                    You poet
                    The Wind Rose

FIN

Al caer la nieve
Puso blancas algunas barbas

    Los ojos medio abiertos
    Son pedazos de vidrio
    Pero quedaba siempre
    Un poco de fuego

Cuando vino la muerte   S
Cortó la última silaba   I
Y todos los que lloraban   L
Se fueron separando   E
                                                N
    A lo largo del camino   C
        Había algunas estrellas deshojadas   I
                                                O

Y los cigarros que se alejaban
Entre los árboles
Son fuegos fatuos

END

When falling the snow
Whitened some beards

    His half-open eyes
    Are pieces of glass
    But there was still
    A little fire left

When death came   S
It cut short the final syllable   I
And all those who wept   L
Went their separate ways   E
                                                    N
    Along the path   C
    There were some plucked stars   E

And the cigars that retreated
Amongst the trees
Are will 'o the wisps

NOTES

Horizon carré was Huidobro's biggest book at the time of its publication, and marked his entry into the world of French poetry. The *mise-en-page* clearly shows the influence of Apollinaire, who had befriended Huidobro at an early stage in Paris, and there are also influences from Pierre Reverdy, although the latter would later reject his own work from this period as a false step. Reverdy assisted Huidobro with some of the French versions, as did (more frequently) the Spanish painter, Juan Gris.

The book was published by Pierre Birault in Paris in 1917, but only properly distributed in Spring 1918, and was never reprinted, although some of the poems reappeared in the author's later selected volume, *Saisons choisies*, in 1921. Birault (1872-1918) was a kind of house publisher to the avant-garde at that time, and had issued three volumes of Reverdy's work, each also containing graphics by Matisse.

At this time all the avant-gardes were busy issuing manifestos, starting journals, holding exhibitions and other public events, and all were interested in the latest *-isms*. The literary scene in which Huidobro found himself was allied to Cubism in the visual arts and, at first, "literary Cubism" was spoken of. Huidobro came up with his own variant, *Creationism*, in which Reverdy was briefly a fellow "member", as was the Spanish poet, Gerardo Diego. To all intents and purposes, Creationism was however more of a mask for Huidobro himself, and attempts to attract others (barring, for a while, Diego) led to nothing. Other writers in Spain quickly donned a new mantle—that of Ultraism, with its attendant magazine, *Ultra*. The main members (1918-1922) were Rafael Cansinos Assens, an early acquaintance of Huidobro's in Madrid, Guillermo de Torre, Juan Larrea, Gerardo Diego and Jorge Luis Borges, then resident in Madrid. Larrea in particular continued to be a close associate and supporter of Huidobro. The intellectual scene of the era, reflected in international Dada, in Italian Futurism, in Russian Cubo-Futurism and *zaum* writing, in Spanish Ultraism, and then in French Surrealism, was febrile. Old orders were being overthrown, just as they were in the political arena, where the old regimes vanished and empires collapsed.

Whatever else may have been happening, Huidobro must have felt as if the whole literary world was shifting under his feet. He quickly found a sense of equilibrium, however, and *Horizon carré*—notwithstanding the substantial contributions of Gris and Reverdy, among others, set down a marker. Together with the other collections from the 1917-1918 period (which are collected in two separate volume in this series)—*El espejo de agua* (in Spanish), *Ecuatorial* (in Spanish), *Tour Eiffel* (in French), *Hallali* (in French) and *Poemas árticos* (in Spanish), this book signals an enormous shift in sensibility, and a decisive move away from his recent *modernista* style, of which some traces still remain in *El espejo de agua*, a chapbook collection which narrowly antedates the author's arrival in Europe but which represents his first significant mature work.

The Text

The layouts here follow those of the first edition—thanks to a PDF of that edition being made available for download by the Fundación Vicente Huidobro in 2016. In cases where a decision as to the correct layout was in doubt, the 2003 *Obra poética* was the arbiter, containing, as it does, a number of manuscript variants. Nothing is definitive, however, and, while I can defend all the choices I have made as to to lineation and spacing, there will be some who will hold other views. *In general* I have followed the 1917 edition, but have over-ridden it in cases of carried-over lines and also stepped lines that seem to start too far left, mostly due, I believe, to restrictions caused by the edition's right-hand margin. I have also added accents to capitalised French words that lacked them in the original; capitalisation at the beginnings of lines or phrases is erratic in the original and I have not interfered with this, except in one case in a Spanish version, where it seemed to be that the *Obra poética* was most likely in error.

The first section of *Horizon carré* is mostly drawn from Huidobro's earlier Spanish-language volume *El espejo de agua* (The Water Mirror) in versions that are by the author but which have clearly benefited from extensive interventions by his friends with better (or, indeed, native) French.

'L'homme triste' is a version by Pierre Reverdy of 'El hombre triste' in *El espejo de agua* (henceforward referred to as EdA). It first appeared in Reverdy's *Nord-Sud* 2 in 1917.

'L'homme gai' is a French version, with a new layout, of 'El hombre alegre' in EdA.

'Automne' is a French version, with a new layout, of 'Otoño' in EdA.

'Minuit' is a French version, with a new layout, of 'Nocturno' in EdA.

'Noir' is a French version, with a new layout, of 'Nocturno II' in EdA.

'Nouvel an' is a French version, with a new layout, of 'Año nuevo' in EdA.

'Âme' is a French version, with a new layout, of 'Alguien iba a nacer' in EdA.

* * *

The Spanish versions in the final part of this book require some explanations; all are from manuscripts in the author's hand, and the source for the transcriptions is the 2003 *Obra poética*.

'Nueva canción' is one of three manuscript versions of a translation of 'Nouvelle chanson'; this version is the closest to the original French, but still has some minor differences.

'Espejo' is a translation of 'Glace', and replaces the poem 'El espejo de agua' from EdA.

'El hombre triste' here is the Spanish version of the French translation, mostly retaining the layout thereof rather than using the left-adjusted orientation of the original in EdA.

'El hombre alegre' here is the Spanish version of the French translation of the poem of the same name, originally printed in EdA, but mostly retaining the French layout.

'Paisaje' is a translation of 'Paysage', but is shorter, and laid out slightly differently.

'[Aeroplano]', which lacks a formal title in the manuscript, is a translation of 'Aéroplane', slightly more compressed than the original.

'Fábula' is a translation of 'Fable', with a more traditional textual organisation, and some minor lexical differences.

'[Río]' which also lacks a formal title in the manuscript, is a translation of 'Fleuve', but abandons the capitalisation of the original and shows some minor differences at the end of the poem.

'Mañana' is a translation of 'Matin', and has lost only two oblique lines from near the beginning of the poem.

'Guitarra' is a translation of 'Guitare', with only a few minor differences from the French original.

'Vates' is a translation of the eponymous French poem, but is much shorter.

'Fin' is a translation of 'Fin', but has a few differences of layout.

Tony Frazer

www.ingramcontent.com/pod-product-compliance
Lightning Source LLC
Chambersburg PA
CBHW030901170426
43193CB00009BA/702